KU-411-397

With every blessing
and gratitude.

Christmas, 1998.

Δ. Sloss.

ANGELS

ANGELS

AN ANTHOLOGY
OF VERSE AND PROSE

LORENZ BOOKS

First published in 1995 by Lorenz Books

© Anness Publishing Limited

Lorenz Books is an imprint of
Anness Publishing Limited
Boundary Row Studios
1 Boundary Row
London SE1 8HP

All rights reserved. No part of this publication may be
reproduced, stored in a retrieval system, or transmitted in
any way or by any means, electronic, mechanical,
photocopying, recording or otherwise, without the prior
permission of the copyright holder.

ISBN 1 85967 105 5

A CIP catalogue record is available from the British Library

Editorial Director: Joanna Lorenz
Project Editor: Joanne Rippin
Consultant Editor: Steve Dobell
Designer: Janet James

Printed and bound by Star Standard, Singapore

CONTENTS

CHAPTER ONE

Dear and Great Angel

Dear and great Angel, wouldst thou only leave
  That child, when thou hast done with him, for me!
Let me sit all the day here, that when eve
  Shall find performed thy special ministry,
And time come for departure, thou, suspending
Thy flight, mayst see another child for tending,
  Another still, to quiet and retrieve.

ROBERT BROWNING *The Guardian-Angel*

THERE are two angels, that attend unseen
Each one of us, and in great books record
Our good and evil deeds. He who writes down
The good ones, after every action closes
His volume, and ascends with it to God.
The other keeps his dreadful day-book open
Till sunset, that we may repent; which doing,
The record of the action fades away,
And leaves a line of white across the page.

HENRY WADSWORTH LONGFELLOW *Christus*

I dreamt a dream! What can it mean?
And that I was a maiden Queen
Guarded by an Angel mild:
Witless woe was ne'er beguiled!

And I wept both night and day,
And he wiped my tears away;
And I wept both day and night,
And hid from him my heart's delight.

So he took his wings and fled;
Then the morn blushed rosy red.
I dried my tears, and armed my fears
With ten thousand shields and spears.

Soon my Angel came again;
I was armed, he came in vain;
For the time of youth was fled,
And grey hairs were on my head.

WILLIAM BLAKE *The Angel*

Abou ben Adhem (may his tribe increase)
Awoke one night from a deep dream of peace,
And saw, within the moonlight in his room,
Making it rich, and like a lily in bloom,
An angel, writing in a book of gold: –
Exceeding peace had made Ben Adhem bold,
And to the presence in the room he said,
'What writest thou?' – The vision raised its head,
And, with a look made of all sweet accord,
Answered, 'The names of those who love the Lord.'
'And is mine one?' said Abou. 'Nay, not so,'
Replied the angel. Abou spoke more low,
But cheerly still; and said, 'I pray thee, then,
Write me as one that loves his fellow-men.'

The angel wrote, and vanished. The next night
It came again with a great wakening light,
And showed the names whom love of God had blessed,
And lo! Ben Adhem's name led all the rest.

LEIGH HUNT *Abou ben Adhem and the Angel*

A poor – torn heart – a tattered heart –
That sat it down to rest –
Nor noticed that the Ebbing Day
Flowed silver to the West –
Nor noticed Night did soft descend –
Nor Constellation burn –
Intent upon the vision
Of latitudes unknown.

The angels – happening that way
This dusty heart espied –
Tenderly took it up from toil
And carried it to God –
There – sandals for the Barefoot –
There – gathered from the gales –
Do the blue havens by the hand
Lead the wandering Sails.

EMILY DICKINSON No. 78 *A Poor, Torn Heart*

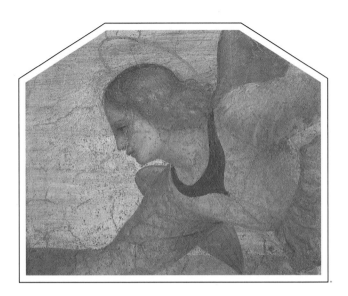

CHAPTER TWO

Winged Heralds

Angels, from the realms of glory,
  Wing your flight o'er all the earth;
Ye who sang creation's story
  Now proclaim Messiah's birth:
    Come and worship,
    Worship Christ, the new-born King.

J MONTGOMERY *Angels, from the Realms of Glory*

And in the sixth month the angel Gabriel was sent from God unto a city of Galilee, named Nazareth, to a virgin espoused to a man whose name was Joseph, of the house of David; and the virgin's name was Mary. And the angel came in unto her, and said, 'Hail, thou that art highly favoured, the Lord is with thee: blessed art thou among women.' And when she saw him, she was troubled at his saying, and cast in her mind what manner of salutation this should be. And the angel said unto her, 'Fear not, Mary: for thou hast found favour with God. And, behold, thou shalt conceive in thy womb, and bring forth a son, and shalt call his name Jesus. He shall be great, and shall be called the Son of the Highest: and the Lord God shall give unto him the throne of his father David; and he shall reign over the house of Jacob for ever; and of his kingdom there shall be no end.'

The Gospel according to Saint Luke, Ch1 v:26–33

IF the Celestials daily fly
With messages on missions high,
And float, our nests and turrets nigh,
    Conversing on Heaven's great intents;
What wonder hints of coming things,
Whereto men's hope and yearning clings,
Should drop like feathers from their wings
    And give us vague presentiments.

JEAN INGELOW from *Scholar and Carpenter*

ENOUGH for him, whom cherubim
   Worship night and day,
A breastful of milk,
   And a mangerful of hay;
Enough for him, whom angels
   Fall down before,
The ox and ass and camel
   Which adore.

Angels and archangels
   May have gathered there,
Cherubim and seraphim
   Thronged the air:
But only his mother
   In her maiden bliss
Worshipped the Belovèd
   With a kiss.

CHRISTINA ROSSETTI
In the Bleak Mid-Winter

LITTLE Jesus, was Thou shy
Once, and just so small as I?
And what did it feel like to be
Out of Heaven, and just like me?
Didst Thou sometimes think of *there*,
And ask where all the angels were?
I should think that I would cry
For my house all made of sky;
I would look about the air,
And wonder where my angels were;
And at waking 'twould distress me –
Not an angel there to dress me!

Hadst Thou ever any toys,
Like us little girls and boys?
And didst Thou play in Heaven with all
The angels, that were not too tall,
With stars for marbles? Did the things
Play 'Can you see me?' through their wings?

FRANCIS THOMPSON *Ex Ore Infantium*

CHAPTER THREE

Bright Squadrons

AND their bright squadrons round
about us plant;
And all for love and nothing for reward:

EDMUND SPENSER *The Ministry of Angels*

AND is there care in Heaven? And is there love
In heavenly spirits to these creatures base,
That may compassion of their evils move?
There is: – else much more wretched were the case
Of men than beasts: but O! th'exceeding grace
Of highest God, that loves his creatures so,
And all his works with mercy doth embrace,
That blessed angels he sends to and fro,
To serve to wicked man, to serve his foe!

How oft do they their silver bowers leave
To come to succour us that succour want!
How oft do they with golden pinions cleave
The flitting skies, like flying pursuivant,
Against foul fiends to aid us militant!
They for us fight, they watch and duly ward,
And their bright squadrons round about us plant;
And all for love and nothing for reward:
O, why should heavenly God to men have such regard?

EDMUND SPENSER *The Ministry of Angels*

Aɴᴅ there was war in heaven: Michael and his angels fought against the dragon; and the dragon fought and his angels, and prevailed not; neither was their place found any more in heaven. And the great dragon was cast out, that old serpent, called the Devil, and Satan, which deceiveth the whole world: he was cast out into the earth, and his angels were cast out with him.

AND I saw an angel come down from heaven, having the key of the bottomless pit and a great chain in his hand. And he laid hold on the dragon, that old serpent, which is the Devil, and Satan, and bound him a thousand years, and cast him into the bottomless pit, and shut him up, and set a seal upon him, that he should deceive the nations no more, till the thousand years should be fulfilled: and after that he must be loosed a little season.

The Revelation of St John the Divine, ch 12 v: 7–9 and ch 20 v: 1–2

ON a starred night Prince Lucifer uprose.
Tired of his dark dominion swung the fiend
Above the rolling ball in cloud part screened,
Where sinners hugged their spectre of repose.
Poor prey to his hot fit of pride were those.
And now upon his western wing he leaned,
Now his huge bulk o'er Afric's sands careened,
Now the black planet shadowed Arctic snows.
Soaring through wider zones that pricked his scars
With memory of the old revolt from Awe,
He reached a middle height, and at the stars,
Which are the brain of heaven, he looked, and sank.
Around the ancient track marched, rank on rank,
The army of unalterable law.

GEORGE MEREDITH *Lucifer in Starlight*

Now when fair morn orient in heav'n appeared,
Up rose the victor Angels, and to arms
The matin trumpet sung: in arms they stood
Of golden panoply, refulgent host,
Soon banded: others from the dawning hills
Looked round, and scouts each coast light-armèd scour
Each quarter, to descry the distant foe,
Where lodged, or whither fled, or if for fight,
In motion or in halt: him soon they met,
Under spread ensigns moving nigh, in slow
But firm battalion: back with speediest sail
Zophiel, of Cherubim the swiftest wing,
Came flying, and in mid air aloud thus cried:

  'Arm, warriors, arm for fight! the foe at hand,
Whom fled we thought, will save us long pursuit
This day; fear not his flight; so thick a cloud
He comes, and settled in his face I see
Sad resolution and secure: let each
His adamantine coat gird well, and each
Fit well his helm, gripe fast his orbèd shield,
Borne ev'n or high; for this day will pour down,
If I conjecture aught, no drizzling show'r,
But rattling storm of arrows barbed with fire.'

JOHN MILTON *Paradise Lost*

CHAPTER FOUR

I Sat With Love

I sat with Love upon a woodside well,
  Leaning across the water, I and he;

DANTE GABRIEL ROSSETTI *Willow-Wood*

I sat with Love upon a woodside well,
   Leaning across the water, I and he;
   Now ever did he speak or look at me,
But touched his lute wherein was audible
The certain secret thing he had to tell:
   Only our mirrored eyes met silently
   In the low wave; and that sound came to be
The passionate voice I knew; and my tears fell.

And at their fall, his eyes beneath grew hers;
And with his foot and with his wing-feathers
   He swept the spring that watered my heart's drouth.
Then the dark ripples spread to the waving hair,
And as I stooped, her own lips rising there
   Bubbled with brimming kisses at my mouth.

DANTE GABRIEL ROSSETTI *Willow-Wood*

WHY was Cupid a boy?
  And why a boy was he?
He should have been a girl,
  For aught that I can see.

For he shoots with his bow,
  And the girl shoots with her eye;
And they both are merry and glad,
  And laugh when we do cry.

Then to make Cupid a boy
  Was surely a woman's plan,
For a boy never learns so much
  Till he has become a man.

And then he's so pierced with cares,
  And wounded with arrowy smarts,
That the whole business of his life
  Is to pick out the heads of the darts.

WILLIAM BLAKE *Cupid*

PLACE the helm on thy brow,
    In thy hand take the spear;
Thou art arm'd, Cupid, now,
    And thy battle-hour is near.
March on! march on! thy shaft and bow
    Were weak against such charms;
March on! march on! so proud a foe
    Scorns all but martial arms.

See the darts in her eyes,
    Tipt with scorn, how they shine!
Ev'ry shaft, as it flies,
    Mocking proudly at thine.
March on! march on! thy feather'd darts
    Soft bosoms soon might move;
But ruder arms to ruder hearts
    Must teach what 'tis to love.
Place the helm on thy brow;
    In thy hand take the spear, –
Thou art arm'd, Cupid, now,
    And thy battle-hour is near.

THOMAS MOORE *Cupid Armed*

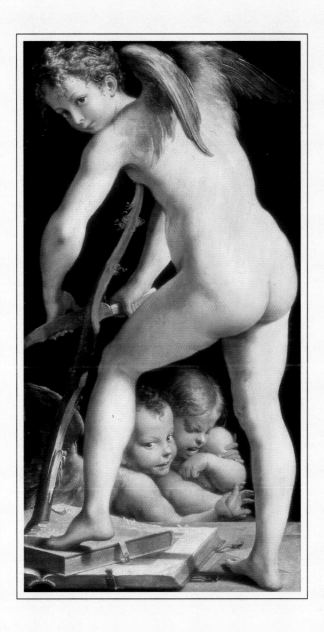

Aɴᴅ feeble, exhausted, unawares she took
To gazing on the god, – till, look by look,
   Her eyes with larger life did fill and glow.
She saw his golden head alight with curls, –
     She might have guessed their brightness in the dark
     By that ambrosial smell of heavenly mark!
She saw the milky brow, more pure than pearls,
     The purple of the cheeks, divinely sundered
By the globed ringlets, as they glided free,
Some back, some forwards, – all so radiantly . . .

ELIZABETH BARRETT BROWNING *Psyche Gazing on Cupid*

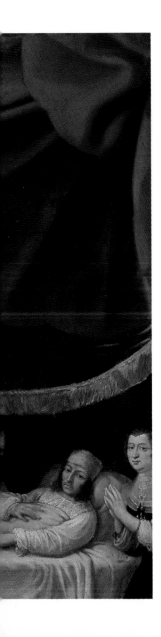

Eros, from rest in isles far-famed,
With rising Anthesterion rose,
And all Hellenic heights acclaimed
   Eros.

The sea one pearl, the shore one rose,
All round him all the flower-month flamed
And lightened, laughing off repose.

Earth's heart, sublime and unashamed,
Knew, even perchance as man's heart knows,
The thirst of all men's nature named
   Eros.

ALGERNON CHARLES SWINBURNE *Eros*

CHAPTER FIVE

A Band of Angels

I looked over Jordan, and what did I see,
Comin' for to carry me home?
A band of angels comin' after me,
Comin' for to carry me home.

ANON

MUSIC the fiercest grief can charm,
And fate's severest rage disarm;
Music can soften pain to ease,
And make despair and madness please:
Our joys below it can improve,
And antedate the bliss above.
This the divine Cecilia found,
And to her Maker's praise confined the sound.
When the full organ joins the tuneful quire,
The immortal powers incline their ear;
Borne on the swelling notes our souls aspire,
While solemn airs improve the sacred fire;
And angels lean from heaven to hear.
Of Orpheus now no more let poets tell,
To bright Cecilia greater power is given;
His numbers raised a shade from hell,
Hers lift the soul to heaven.

ALEXANDER POPE *Ode on St Cecilia's Day*

In Heaven a spirit doth dwell
  'Whose heart-strings are a lute';
None sing so wildly well
As the angel Israfel,
And the giddy stars (so legends tell),
Ceasing their hymns, attend the spell
  Of his voice, all mute.

And they say (the starry choir
  And the other listening things)
That Israfeli's fire
Is owing to that lyre
  By which he sits and sings –
The trembling living wire
  Of those unusual strings.

If I could dwell
Where Israfel
  Hath dwelt, and he where I,
He might not sing so wildly well
  A mortal melody,
While a bolder note than this might swell
  From my lyre within the sky.

EDGAR ALLAN POE *Israfel*

No sooner had th' Almighty ceased, but all
The multitude of angels with a shout,
Loud as from numbers without number, sweet
As from blest voices, uttering joy, heav'n rung
With jubilee, and loud hosannas filled
The eternal regions . . .

Then, crowned again, their golden harps they took,
Harps ever tuned, that glittering by their side
Like quivers hung, and with preamble sweet
Of charming symphony they introduce
Their sacred song, and waken raptures high;
No voice exempt, no voice but well could join
Melodious part, such concord is in heaven.

JOHN MILTON *Paradise Lost*

Angel spirits of sleep,
White-robed, with silver hair,
In your meadows fair,
Where the willows weep,
And the sad moonbeam
On the gliding stream
Writes her scattered dream:

Angel spirits of sleep,
Dancing to the weir
In the hollow roar
Of its waters deep;
Know ye how men say
That ye haunt no more
Isle and grassy shore
With your moonlit play;
That ye dance not here;
White-robed spirits of sleep,
All the summer night
Threading dances light?

ROBERT BRIDGES *Spirits*

CHAPTER SIX

Jubilant Hosts

MORE than a thousand jubilant Angels saw I,
Each differing in effulgence and in kind.

DANTE *Paradiso*

AND at that centre, with their wings expanded,
　　More than a thousand jubilant Angels saw I,
　　Each differing in effulgence and in kind.
I saw there at their sports and at their songs
　　A beauty smiling, which the gladness was
　　Within the eyes of all the other saints;
And if I had in speaking as much wealth
　　As in imagining, I should not dare
　　To attempt the smallest part of its delight.

DANTE *Paradiso*

HARK! the herald Angels sing
Glory to the new-born King.
Peace on earth, and mercy mild,
God and sinners reconciled.
Joyful all ye nations, rise,
Join the triumph of the skies;
With the Angelic host proclaim,
Christ is born in Bethlehem.
　　Hark! the herald Angels sing
　　Glory to the new-born King.

CHARLES WESLEY
Hark, the Herald Angels Sing

MINE Eye doth pierce the heavens, and see
What is Invisible to thee.
My garments are not silk nor gold,
Nor such like trash which Earth doth hold,
But Royal Robes I shall have on,
More glorious than the glistring Sun;
My Crown not Diamonds, Pearls, and Gold,
But such as Angels heads infold.
The City where I hope to dwell,
There's none on Earth can Parallel:
The stately Walls both high and strong,
Are made of pretious Jasper stone;
The Gates of Pearl, both rich and clear,
And Angels are for Porters there;
The Streets thereof transparent gold,
Such as no Eye did e're behold;
A Chrystal River there doth run,
Which doth proceed from the Lamb's Throne.

ANNE BRADSTREET *The Flesh and the Spirit*

Let them praise Thy Name, let them praise Thee, the supercelestial people, Thine angels, who have no need to gaze up at this firmament, or by reading to know of Thy word. For they always behold Thy face, and there read without any syllables in time, what willeth Thy eternal will; they read, they choose, they love. They are ever reading; and that never passes away which they read; for by choosing, and by loving, they read the very unchangeableness of Thy counsel. Their book is never closed, nor their scroll folded up; seeing Thou Thyself art this to them, and art eternally; because Thou hast ordained them above this firmament, which Thou hast firmly settled over the infirmity of the lower people, where they might gaze up and learn Thy mercy, announcing in time Thee Who madest times. For Thy mercy, O Lord, is in the heavens, and Thy truth reacheth unto the clouds. The clouds pass away, but the heaven abideth.

SAINT AUGUSTINE *Confessions*

ACKNOWLEDGEMENTS

The following pictures are reproduced with kind permission of the Bridgeman Art Library, London:

Front jacket: *Angel Musician* by Melozzo da Forli (1438–94) Vatican Museums and Galleries, Rome. Endpapers: *Triumph of the Hapsburgs* by Luca Giordano (1632–1705) Monasterio de El Escorial, Spain. p1 *Angel* by Sir Edward Burne-Jones (1833–98) Private Collection. p2 *Angel* by Abbott Handerson Thayer (1849–1921) National Museum of American Art, Smithsonian Inst. p6 *Adoration of the Shepherds* by Adriaan van der Werff (1659–1722) Galleria degli Uffizi, Florence. p7 *The Angel of Life* by Giovanni Segantini (1858–99) Galleria d'Arte Moderna, Milan. p8 (detail) p12 (detail) p40 (detail) from Ms 209 f.24v The Vintage: angel with sickle ordered by angel to cut the vine, Lambeth Apocalypse (c1260) Lambeth Palace Library. p9 *The Guardian Angels* by Joshua Hargrave Sams Mann (fl.1849–85) Haynes Fine Art at the Bindery Galleries, Broadway. p11 *Study for Homer's Apotheosis* by Jean-Auguste Dominique Ingres (1780–1867) Musee Bonnat, Bayonne. p13 *Dream of St Ursula* by Vittore Carpaccio (c1460/1523/6) Galleria dell'Accademia, Venice. p14 *Untitled; a woman adrift in a boat guided by Guardian Angels* by Anonymous, Forbes Magazine Collection/London. p15 *Christ in the Sepulchre, Guarded by Angels* by William Blake (1757–1827) Victoria and Albert Museum, London. p16 *Angel* (fresco) by Bernardino Luini (1480–1532) Pinacoteca di Brera, Milan. p17 *Triumph of the Hapsburgs* by Luca Giordano (1632–1705) Monasterio de El Escorial, Spain. p18 *Annuciation* by Filippino Lippi (c1457/8–1504) Galleria dell'Accademia, Florence. p19 *The Annunciation, Panel from the Main Altarpiece in Palencia Cathedral* by Juan de Flandres (fl 1496–c1519) Castilla Leon, Palencia/Index. p20 *Cherubs, from the Adoration of the Shepherds* by Philippe de Champaigne (1602–74) Wallace Collection, London. p21 (top) *Amorini* (red chalk) by Francois Boucher (1703–70) (follower of) Wallace Collection, London. p21 (bottom) *Nativity* by Charles Poerson (1609–67) Louvre, Paris/Giraudon. p22/23 *Christ, St John and two Angels* by Peter Paul Rubens (1577–1640) Collection of the Earl of Pembroke, Wilton House. p24 Ms65/1284 f.64v Fall of the rebel angels Tres Riches Heures du Duc de Berry (early 15th c) Musee Conde, Chantilly. p25 *The Fall of the Rebel Angels* by Sebastiano Ricci (1658–1734) Dulwich Picture Gallery, London. p26 *Angel with a Sword* (oak panel) by Hans Memling (fl 1465-d 1495) Wallace Collection, London. p27 Detail of Angels from the Altarpiece of St Barnabas by Sandro Botticelli (1444/5–1510) Galleria degli Uffizi, Florence. p28 *St Michael and the Devil* by Raffaello Sanzio Raphael of Urbino (1483–1520) Louvre, Paris/Giraudon. p29 (top, detail) *Tobias and the Archangel Raphael* by Francesco Botticini (c1446–97) Sacristy of Florence Cathedral. p29 (bottom) Ms 209 f35 Angel drags chained dragon away to prison, Lambeth Apocalypse (c1260) Lambeth Palace Library, London. p30 *Concert of Angels, detail from the Isenheim Altarpiece* by Mattias Grunewald (1455–1528) Unterlinden Museum, Colmar, France. p31 *Fall of Satan and the Rebel Angels from Heaven by Jakob Swanenburgh (1571–1638)* Rafael Valls Gallery, London. p32 *The Ascension of Christ* (fresco) by Jacopo Tintoretto

(1518–94) Scuola Grande di San Rocco, Venice. p34 *Benedicite No 1 'O all ye green things upon earth', 1899* by Edward A Fellowes Prynne (1854–1921) Russell-Cotes Art Gallery and Museum, Bournemouth. p35 *The Ramparts of God's House* by John Melhuish Strudwick (1849–1937) Christie's, London. p36 (detail) *Angels at the Annunciation* by Francesco Granacci (1477–1543) Galleriea dell'Accademia, Florence. p37 *Two Angels* by Charles Francois Sellier (1830–82) Private Collection. p38 Cupid an Psyche by Annie Swynnerton (1844–1933) Oldham Art Gallery, Lancs. p39 *Cupidon, 1891* by William-Adolphe Bouguereau (1825–1905) Roy Miles Gallery, 29 Bruton Street, London W1. p41 *Cupid Carving a Bow* by Francesco (Mazzola) Parmigianino (1503–40) Kunsthistorisches Museum, Vienna/Ali Meyer. p42 (left) *Cupid: on Guard* by Thomas Stothard (1755–1834) Simon Carter Gallery, Woodbridge. p43/43 *Cupid and Psyche* by Paolo di Matteis (1662–1728) Christie's, London. p44/45 Votive offering of Louis XIV by Nicolas Mignard (1606–68) Chateau de Versailles, France/Giraudon. p46 *Four Angels Playing Instruments* by Taborda Vlame Carlos (16th century) National Museum of Ancient Art, Lisbon/Giraudon. p47 *Aurora Ascending the Heavens* by Julien de Parme (1736–99) Prado, Madrid. p48 *Angel* by Sir Edward Burne-Jones (1833–98) Private Collection. p49 *The Dream of St Cecilia* by Paul Baudry (1828–86) Musee des Beaux-Arts, Moulins/Giraudon. p50 (top right) *Angel playing the Lute* by Giovanni Battista Rosso (1494–1540) Galleria Degli Uffizi, Florence. p51 *Angels, from the Side Walls in the Chapel* by Benozzo Gozzoli (c1420–97) Palazzo Medici-Riccardi, Florence. p52 *Angeli Laudantes* c1887 by Sir Edward Burne-Jones (1833–98) (design for a window in Salisbury Cathedral, also for tapestries) Fitzwilliam Museum, University of Cambridge. p53 *Angel Playing a Trumpet*, detail from the Linaiuoli Triptych by Fra Angelico (c1387–1455) Museo di San Marco dell'Angelico, Florence. p54 by Abbott Handerson Thayer (1849–1921) National Museum of American Art, Smithsonian Inst. p55 *The Cloister or the World* by Arthur Hacker (1858–1919) Bradford Art Galleries & Museums. p56 *Angels at the Annunciation* by Francesco Granacci (1477–1543) Galleria dell'Accademia, Florence. p57 *Detail of Heaven from the Last Judgement* by Fra Angelico (c1387–1455) Museo di San Marco dell'Angelico, Florence. p58 *Angels Playing Musical Instruments* c1475–97 by Francesco Botticini (c1446–97) (attr) Museo della Collegiata di Sant'Andrea, Empoli. p59 *A Concert of Angels* by Spanish School (16th century) Museo de Bellas Artes, Bilbao/Index. p60 *The Story of Cupid and Psyche* by Jacopo del Sellaio (1441/42–93) Fitzwilliam Museum, University of Cambridge. p61 *An Angel holding a Glass Flask* by Juan de Valdes Leal (1622–90) Phillips, the International Fine Art Auctioneers. p62 *Angels, detail from the Madonna della Melagrana* by Sandro Botticelli (1444/5–1510) Galleria degli Uffizi, Florence. p63 (detail) *Aurora Ascending the Heavens by Julien de Parme (1736–99)* Prado, Madrid. p64 *Madonna Carried by Angels* by Jacopo Palma (Il Giovane) (1544–1628) Oratorio del Crociferi, Venice.

Thanks also to the Mary Evans Picture library for permission to reproduce pictures on back jacket, p33 and p50 (left).